Christmas 1992.

Dear Amy:

A 'treasure' for you to treasure. All our Love

Mom & Dad xxoo

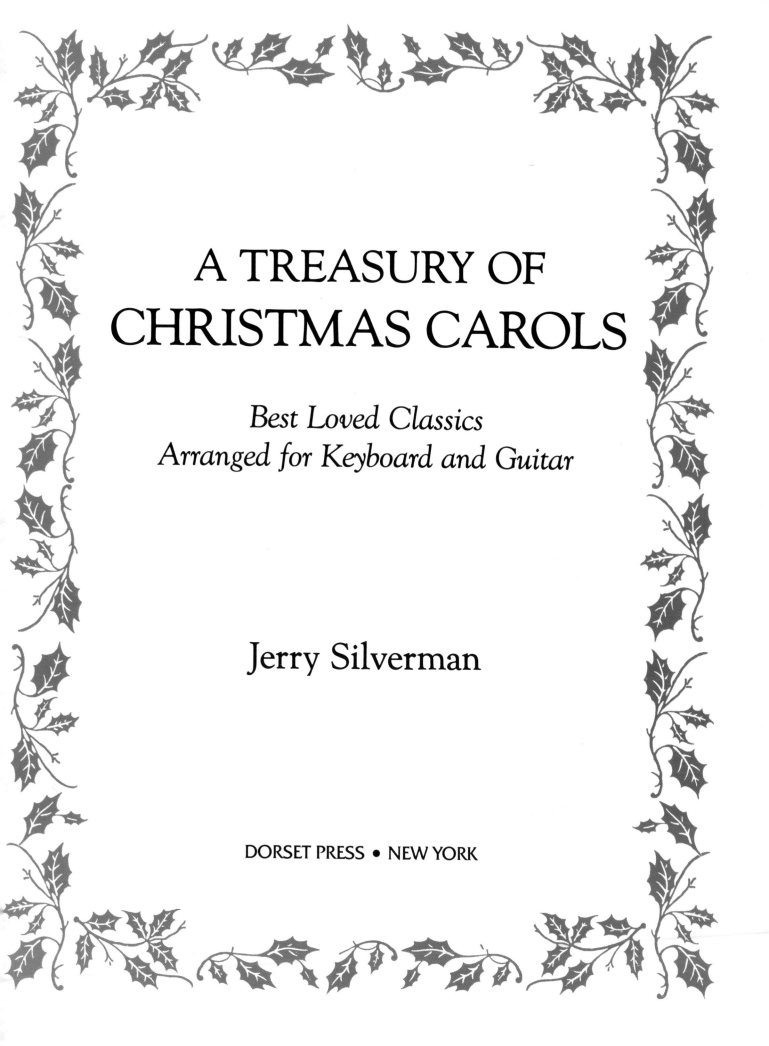

A TREASURY OF CHRISTMAS CAROLS

Best Loved Classics
Arranged for Keyboard and Guitar

Jerry Silverman

DORSET PRESS • NEW YORK

Color illustrations on pages 29, 47, 55 and 67 used by permission
of Art Resource.
The Victorian postcards reproduced throughout this work are
reprinted courtesy of Aaron's Archives.

This edition published by Dorset Press,
a division of Marboro Books Corp.,
by arrangement with Saw Mill Music Corp.
1991 Dorset Press

Printed and bound in Hong Kong

ISBN 0-88029-720-4

M 9 8 7 6 5 4 3 2

Contents

Jingle Bells	4	Go Tell It On The Mountain	50
O Christmas Tree	6	I Saw Three Ships	52
Angels We Have Heard On High	8	Mary Had A Baby	54
Hark! The Herald Angels Sing	10	Good Christian Men, Rejoice	56
We Three Kings Of Orient Are	12	It Was Poor Little Jesus	58
We Wish You A Merry Christmas	14	It Took Place One Christmas Eve	60
The Twelve Days Of Christmas	16	Tonight A Child Is Born	62
A Child Now Is Born In Bethlehem	19	Joyful Sing Ye, Christian People	64
What Child Is This	20	The Virgin Mary Had A Son	66
Joy To The World!	22	Santa Claus Blues	68
O Come, O Come Emmanuel	24	Silent Night, Holy Night	70
The Holly Bears A Berry	26	O Come, All Ye Faithful	72
Once In Royal David's City	28	A Child This Day Is Born	74
Jolly Old Saint Nicholas	30	God Rest You Merry Gentlemen	76
Here We Come A-Wassailing	32	The First Noël	78
Masters In This Hall	34	We All Go To Bethlehem	80
The Seven Blessings of Mary	36	Deck The Halls	82
The Cherry Tree Carol	38	O Little Town Of Bethlehem	84
What Month Was My Jesus Born In?	40	Good King Wenceslas	86
Lo, How A Rose E'er Blooming	42	Away In A Manger	88
Gather Around The Christmas Tree	44	It Came Upon The Midnight Clear	90
O Holy Night	46	O Come Little Children	92
I Heard The Bells On Christmas Day	49	Auld Lang Syne	94

JINGLE BELLS

James Pierpont (1822-1893) wrote *The One Horse Open Shay,* as it was first called, in 1850 for a Boston Sunday School. It was republished in 1859 under its present title, but did not attain its great popularity until the twentieth century. Although Pierpont's father was a fiery Abolitionist minister, he himself wrote songs for the Confederacy. He was the uncle of financier John Pierpont Morgan.

J. Pierpont

Dash - ing through the snow In a one horse o - pen sleigh,

O'er the fields we go Laugh - ing all the way.

Bells on bob - tail ring, Mak - ing spir - its bright, What

CHORUS

Jin-gle bells, jin-gle bells, jin-gle all the way, Oh, what fun it

1.
is to ride in a one-horse o-pen sleigh.

2.
one-horse o-pen sleigh.

—— 2 ——

A day or two ago
I thought I'd take a ride,
And soon Miss Fannie Bright
Was seated by my side;
The horse was lean and lank,
Misfortune seem'd his lot,
He got into a drifted bank,
And then we got upsot! *Chorus*

CHRISTMAS TREE

The evergreen tree is a northern European symbol for eternal life. It is a pre-Christian concept that has found its way into our era as the "Christmas Tree". The melody of this well-known German carol has been borrowed and used over and over for a variety of songs, including, *Maryland, My Maryland*—a testimony to the eternal life of a good tune.

O Christ - mas tree, O Christ - mas tree, With faith - ful leaves un -
O Tan - nen - baum, O Tan - nen - baum, Wie treu sind dei - ne

chang - ing. O chang - ing. Not on - ly green in sum - mer's heat, But
Blätt - ter! Oh Blät - ter! Du grünst nicht nur zur som - mer - zeit, 'Nein

al - so win - ter's snow and sleet, O Christ - mas tree, O
auch im win - ter, wenn es schneit, Oh Tan - nen - baum, Oh

Christ - mas tree, With faith - ful leaves un - chang - ing!
Tan - nen - baum, Wie treu sind dei - ne Blät - ter!

— 2 —

O Christmas tree, O Christmas tree,
Of all the trees most lovely,
O Christmas tree, O Christmas tree,
Of all the trees most lovely,
Each year, you bring to me delight
Gleaming in the Christmas night.
O Christmas tree, O Christmas tree,
Of all the trees most lovely,

Oh, Tannenbaum, Oh, Tannenbaum,
Du kannst mir sehr gefallen!
Oh, Tannenbaum, Oh, Tannenbaum,
Du kannst mir sehr gefallen!
Wie oft hat mich zur Weihnachtszeit
Ein Braum von dir mich hoch erfreut!
Oh, Tannenbaum, Oh, Tannenbaum,
Du kannst mir sehr gefallen!

— 3 —

O Christmas tree, O Christmas tree,
Your leaves will teach me, also,
O Christmas tree, O Christmas tree,
Your leaves will teach me, also,
That hope and love and faithfulness
Are precious things I can possess.
O Christmas tree, O Christmas tree,
Your leaves will teach me, also.

Oh, Tannenbaum, Oh, Tannenbaum,
Dein Kleid soll mich was lehren!
Oh, Tannenbaum, Oh, Tannenbaum,
Dein Kleid soll mich was lehren!
Die Hoffnung und Beständigkeit
Gibt Trost und Kraft zu aller Zeit.
Oh, Tannenbaum, Oh, Tannenbaum,
Du kannst mir sehr gefallen!

A Merry Christmas

NGELS WE HAVE HEARD ON HIGH

In A.D. 129, Pope Telesphorus ordained that the *Gloria in Excelsis* be sung on "the Holy Night of the Nativity of our Lord and Saviour". It is still said or sung, with some variations, in all branches of the church which have not relinquished the use of liturgies.

—— 2 ——

Shepherds, why this jubilee?
Why your joyous strains prolong?
What the gladsome tidings be
Which inspire your heav'nly song?   *Chorus*

—— 3 ——

Come to Bethlehem and see
Him Whose birth the angels sing;
Come, adore on bended knee,
Christ the Lord, the new-born King.   *Chorus*

—— 4 ——

See Him in a manger laid,
Whom the choirs of angels praise;
Mary, Joseph, lend your aid,
While our hearts in love we raise.   *Chorus*

ARK! THE HERALD ANGELS SING

Charles Wesley (1707-1788) was the eighteenth child of the Rector of
Epworth, England. He wrote about 6500 hymns and was considered
"the greatest hymn-writer of all ages" by his contemporaries.
Felix Mendelssohn (1809-1847), who had made many visits to England,
met Wesley's son, John, in London in 1839. John Wesley acquainted
Mendelssohn with his father's poetry and this is the result.

Charles Wesley

Felix Mendelssohn

Hark! the her - ald an - gels sing,— "Glo - ry to the new born King!

Peace on earth, and mer - cy mild,— God and sin - ners rec - on - ciled."

Joy - ful, all ye na - tions rise,— Join the tri - umph of the skies;—

| C | E7 | Am E7 Am | D | G | 1.
C D7 G | 2.
C D7 G |

With th'an-gel -ic host pro-claim, "Christ is__ born in Beth - le - hem."
Hark! the her -ald an - gels sing, "Glo - ry__ to the   new born King!"

—— 2 ——

Christ, by highest heaven adorned;
Christ, the everlasting Lord!
Late in time behold Him come,
Offspring of the Virgin's womb.
Veiled in flesh the Godhead see;
Hail th' incarnate Deity,
Pleased as man with men to dwell,
Jesus, our Emmanuel.
Hark, the herald angels sing,
"Glory to the new-born King."

—— 3 ——

Hail, the heaven-born Prince of Peace!
Hail, the Sun of Righteousness!
Light and life to all He brings,
Risen with healing in His wings.
Mild He lays His glory by,
Born that man no more may die.
Born to raise the sons of earth,
Born to give them second birth.
Hark, the herald angels sing,
"Glory to the new-born King."

E THREE KINGS OF ORIENT ARE

The name Hopkins figures prominently in Anglo-American hymnology. The American branch is represented by John Henry Hopkins (1820-1891) who was the son of the second Bishop of Vermont. He was a poet, composer, musicologist and parish rector. He also designed stained-glass windows.

John H. Hopkins

We three Kings of O - ri - ent are; Bear - ing
gifts we trav - erse a - far, Field and foun - tain,
moor and moun - tain, Fol - low - ing yon - der star.

CHORUS

O,_____ star of won - der, star of night,

Star with roy - al beau - ty bright, West - ward lead - ing,

still pro - ceed - ing, Guide us to thy per - fect light.

— 2 —

Born a King on Bethlehem's plain,
Gold I bring, to crown Him again,
King forever, ceasing never,
Over us all to reign.   *Chorus*

— 4 —

Myrrh is mine, it's bitter perfume
Breathes a life of gathering gloom;
Sorrowing, sighing, bleeding, dying,
Sealed in the stone-cold tomb.   *Chorus*

— 3 —

Frankincense to offer have I,
Incense owns a Deity nigh.
Prayer and praising all men raising,
Worship Him God most High.   *Chorus*

— 5 —

Glorious now behold Him arise,
King and God and sacrifice,
Alleluia, Alleluia;
Earth to the heav'ns replies.   *Chorus*

E WISH YOU A MERRY CHRISTMAS

This lively, traditional English Christmas song is perfect to sing while wassailing. (If you don't remember what that means, take a look at *Here We Come A-Wassailing*.)

G   C   A7   D7

We Wish you a mer-ry Christ-mas, we wish you a mer-ry Christ-mas, we

B7   C   D7   G

wish you a mer-ry Christ-mas and a hap-py New Year.

14

—— 2 ——

We all want some figgy pudding,
We all want some figgy pudding,
We all want some figgy pudding,
And a cup of good cheer.

—— 3 ——

We won't go until we get some,
We won't go until we get some,
We won't go until we get some,
So bring it right here.

—— 4 ——

We all know that Santa's coming,
We all know that Santa's coming,
We all know that Santa's coming,
And soon will be here.

THE TWELVE DAYS OF CHRISTMAS

1. On the first day of Christ - mas my true love gave to me a

par - tridge— in a pear tree.

2. On the sec - ond
3. On the third ⎱ day of Christ - mas my
4. On the fourth ⎰

true love gave to me

two tur - tle doves,
three French hens, ⎱ And a
four call - ing birds, ⎰

(Repeat as needed)

par - trige in a pear tree. *D. S.* 5. On the fifth day of Christ-mas my

true love gave to me *CODA* five gold— rings, four— call-ing birds,

three French hens, two— tur-tle doves, And a par-tridge— in a pear tree. *Fine*

(over)

Wishing You a Merry Christmas!

Dal Coda ✛
(al Fine after verse 12)

6. On the sixth
7. On the seventh
8. On the eighth
9. On the ninth ⎫day of Christ-mas my true love gave to me
10. On the tenth
11. On the eleventh
12. On the twelfth ⎭

Six geese a - lay - ing,
Sev- en swans a-swim-ming,
Eight maids a - milk-ing,
Nine la - dies danc-ing,
Ten lords a - leap-ing,
Elev- en pip- ers pip-ing,
Twelve drummers drumming,

How many gifts do you suppose "my true love" actually gave "to me"?
See if you can work it out. Then check your answer on page 81.

CHILD NOW IS BORN IN BETHLEHEM

Lucas Lossius (1508-1582) was the compiler of a comprehensive collection of liturgical music for the use of the Lutheran Church in Germany. The compilation, published in Nuremburg in 1553, contained this song with its Latin title: *Puer natus in Bethlehem.* In 1724, J.S. Bach set this same melody as a four-part chorale in his Cantata 65, *Sie werden aus Saba alle kommen.* This is Bach's choral setting, with the melody extracted as a solo line.

J. S. Bach

A child now is born in Beth - le - hem,
Three Kings came from She - ba by _____ the star,

Beth - le - hem. Re - joice you now, Je - ru - sa -
by _____ the star, With in - cense, gold and myrrh from a -

lem. Al - le - lu - ja, Al - le - lu - ja!
far.

WHAT CHILD IS THIS

William Chatterton Dix (1837-1898), Victorian English hymn writer knew a good tune when he heard one. He set his text to the melody of *Greensleeves*, which itself was first printed in 1580. The concept of setting a Victorian hymn to an Elizabethan song about a lady of somewhat dubious repute has its echo in the choice of the Old English drinking song, *To Anachreon In Heaven*, to bear the words of *The Star-Spangled Banner*.

William C. Dix

What Child is this, who, laid to rest on Mar- y's lap is sleep - ing? Whom an - gels greet with an - thems sweet, While shep - herds watch are keep - ing?

CHORUS

This, this___ is Christ the King, ___ Whom shep - herds guard___ and
Raise, raise___ the song on high, ___ The Vir - gin sings___ her

an - gels sing: Haste, haste___ to bring Him laud,___ the
lul - la - by. Joy, joy,___ for Christ is born,___ the

1. 2.

Final ending

Babe, ___ the Son ___ of Ma - ry.
Babe, ___ the Son ___ of Ma - ry. Ma - ry.

— 2 —

— 3 —

Why lies He in such mean estate,
Where ox and ass are feeding?
Good Christian fear, for sinners here,
The silent word is pleading. *Chorus*

So bring Him incense, gold and myrrh,
Come, peasant kind, to own Him.
The King of kings salvation brings,
Let loving hearts enthrone Him. *Chorus*

JOY TO THE WORLD!

Isaac Watts (1674-1748) was an English theologian and hymn-writer. His hymns, which approach a very high standard of excellence, are at the same time suitable for congregational use. This is his adaptation of Psalm 98, set to music by that naturalized Englishman, George Frederick Handel (1685-1759).

Isaac Watts

George Frederick Handel

Joy to the world! the Lord is come; Let earth re - ceive her King, _____ Let ev - 'ry _ heart _ pre - pare _ Him _ room, _ And heav'n and na - ture _ sing, _____ And _ heav'n and na - ture sing, _____ And

Christmas Greetings.

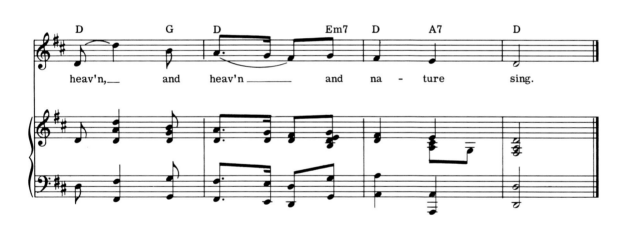

heav'n,___ and heav'n_____ and na - ture sing.

—— 2 ——

Joy to the world! the Saviour reigns;
Let men their songs employ,
While fields and floods,
Rocks, hills, and plains
Repeat the sounding joy,
Repeat the sounding joy,
Repeat, repeat the sounding joy.

—— 3 ——

He rules the world with truth and grace,
And makes the nations prove
The glories of
His righteousness,
The wonders of His love,
The wonders of His love,
The wonders, the wonders of His love.

O COME, O COME EMMANUEL

Thomas Helmore (1811-1890), English clergyman and church musician. He composed and arranged music for some of John N. Neale's translations of *Hymns for the Eastern Church. Veni, Emmanuel,* which can be traced back to a twelfth-century Plain Song, was one of those translations.

Thomas Helmore

O come, O come Em - man - u - el, And ran - som cap - tive
Ve - ni, ve - ni Em - man - u - el, Cap - ti - vum sol - ve

Is - ra - el, That mourns in lone - ly ex - ile
Is - ra - el, Qui ge - mit in ex - i - li -

here Un - til the Son of God ap - pear.
o, Pri - va - tus, De - i fi - li - a

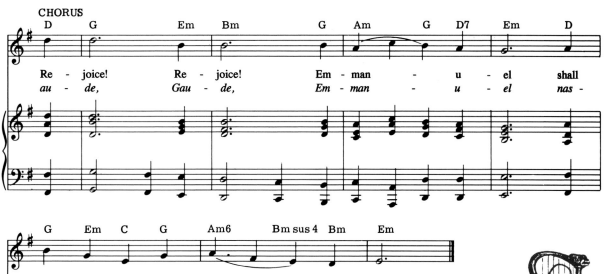

Re - joice! Re - joice! Em - man - u - el shall
au - de, *Gau - de,* *Em - man - u - el nas -*

come to thee O Is - ra - el.
ce - tur po - te Is - ra - el.

—— 2 ——

O come, O come, Thou Rod of Jesse, free
Thine own from Satan's tyranny;
From depths of hell Thy people save,
And give them victory o'er the grave.   *Chorus*

Veni, O Iesse virgula,
Ex hostis tuos ungula,
De specu tuos Tartari
Educ, et antro barathri.   *Chorus*

—— 3 ——

O come, Thou Dayspring, come and cheer
Our spirits by Thine advent here;
Disperse the gloomy clouds of night,
And death's dark shadows put to flight.   *Chorus*

Veni, veni, O Oriens,
Solare nos adveniens:
Noctis depelle nebulas,
Dirasque noctis tenebras.   *Chorus*

—— 4 ——

O come, Thou Key of David, come,
And open wide our heav'nly home;
Make safe the way that leads on high,
And close the path to misery.   *Chorus*

Veni, clavis Davidica,
Regna reclude caelica,
Fac iter tutum superum,
Et claude vias inferum.   *Chorus*

—— 5 ——

O come, O come, Thou Lord of might,
Who once, from Sinai's flaming height
Didst give the trembling tribes Thy law,
In cloud, and majesty, and awe.   *Chorus*

Veni, veni, Adonai,
Qui populo in Sinai
Legem dedisti vertice,
In maiestate gloriae.   *Chorus*

THE HOLLY BEARS A BERRY

This version of the traditional English Christmas carol, *The Holly and the Ivy,* was brought to this country from Australia, where it was collected by folklorist John Greenway in the early 1960's.

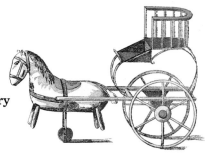

Oh, the hol – ly bears a ber – ry as white as the milk, Ma –

ry bore__ Je – sus all wrap – ped in silk.

CHORUS

Ma – ry bore Je – sus, our Sa – viour to be, And the

first tree in the green-wood it was the hol - ly, hol - ly, hol -

ly, And the first tree in the green - wood it was the hol - ly.

——— 2 ———

Oh, the holly bears a berry
That's green as the grass.
Mary bore Jesus,
Who died on the cross. *Chorus*

——— 3 ———

Oh, the holly bears a berry
As blood it is red.
Mary bore Jesus,
Who died in our stead. *Chorus*

——— 4 ———

Oh, the holly bears a berry
As black as the coal.
Mary bore Jesus,
Who died for us all. *Chorus*

ONCE IN ROYAL DAVID'S CITY

Henry John Gauntlett (1805-1876), English lawyer and organist. In 1844 he drew attention to the subject of Gregorian music by the publication of the *Hymnal for Matins and Evensong.* He was chosen by Mendelssohn to play the organ part in *Elijah* at its production in 1846. He is best remembered as a composer and editor of psalm and hymn tunes.

C. F. Alexander

H. J. Gauntlett

—— 2 ——

He came down to earth from heaven,
Who is God and Lord of all,
And His shelter was a stable,
And His cradle was a stall.
With the poor and mean and lowly,
Lived on earth our Saviour holy.

—— 3 ——

And our eyes at last shall see Him,
Through His own redeeming love,
For that Child so dear and gentle
Is our Lord in heaven above.
And He leads His children on
To the place where He is gone.

JOLLY OLD SAINT NICHOLAS

Operating under the principle that if you don't ask you might not get anything, our young friend has adopted the direct approach. Too bad the stocking is the shortest one. Oh well, wait 'til next year...

Jol - ly old Saint Nich - o - las, Lean your ear this way!

Don't you tell a sin - gle soul What I'm going to say.

Christ - mas Eve is com - ing soon; Now you dear old man,

Christmas Wishes

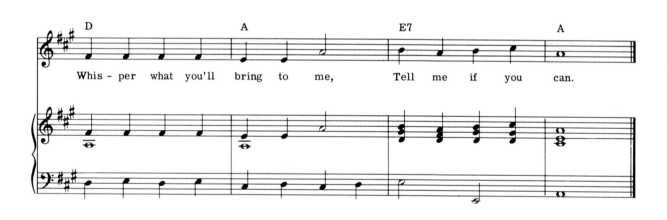

Whis-per what you'll bring to me, Tell me if you can.

— 2 —

When the clock is striking twelve,
When I'm fast asleep,
Down the chimney broad and black,
With your pack you'll creep;
All the stockings you will find
Hanging in a row;
Mine will be the shortest one,
You'll be sure to know.

HERE WE COME A-WASSAILING

Wassail, from the Old English *woes hal*, "be whole, be well", was the ancient form of "toasting", the term being applied later to the Christmas feasting and revelries and particularly to the bowl of spiced ale or wine which was a feature of the medieval Christmas. What was popularly known as wassailing was the custom of trimming with sprigs of rosemary and ribbons a bowl which was carried around the streets by young girls singing carols at Christmas and New Year.

Here we come a - was - sail - ing A - mong the leaves of green;

Here we come a - wan - d'ring so fair to be seen.

Love and joy come to you, And to you your was - sail too; And God

bless you and send__ you a Hap - py New__ Year, And God

send you a Hap - py New__ Year. ____

—— 2 ——

We are not daily beggars
That beg from door to door;
But we are neighbors' children
Whom you have seen before. *Chorus*

—— 3 ——

We have got a little purse,
Of stretching leather skin;
We want a little of your money
To line it well within. *Chorus*

—— 4 ——

Bring us out a table,
And spread it with a cloth;
Bring us out a mouldy cheese,
And some of your Christmas loaf. *Chorus*

—— 5 ——

God bless the master of this house,
Likewise the mistress too;
And all the little children
That 'round the table go. *Chorus*

ASTERS IN THIS HALL

William Morris (1834-1896), English poet and artist. His interests were wide-ranging, and included the decorative arts, architecture and Socialism. He wrote rallying songs for *Commonweal,* the organ of the Socialist League, founded in 1885. He was also taken up with the Victorian Gothic revival, and it is due to that interest that we owe this carol, based on an old French melody.

Mas-ters in this hall, —— Hear ye news to-day, ——

Brought from o - ver - sea, And ev - er I you pray.

Now-ell, Now-ell, Now-ell! Now-ell sing we { clear! Hol - pen are all folk on
{ loud! God to - day hath all folk

earth,___ Born___ is God's Son, so dear.
raised___ And___ cast a-down the proud.

—— 2 ——

Then to Bethl'em town
We went two and two,
In a sorry place
We heard the oxen low. *Chorus*

—— 3 ——

Ox and ass Him know
Kneeling on their knee
Wond'rous joy had I
This little Babe to see. *Chorus*

—— 4 ——

This is Christ, the Lord,
Masters be ye glad!
Christmas is come in
And no folk should be sad. *Chorus*

THE SEVEN BLESSINGS OF MARY

An older version of this carol comes down to us from the mystery plays of fifteenth century England and France. It is a typical "counting song".

The ver-y first bless-ing that Mar-y had, It was the bless-ing of one,_____ To know that her Son, Je - sus, Was God's on-ly Son,_____ Was God's on - ly

CHORUS

Son. Come all ye to the wil-der-ness,

Glo-ry, glo-ry be, Fa-ther, Son, and the

Ho-ly Ghost, Through all e-ter-ni-ty.

The second blessing that Mary had,
It was the blessing of two,
To know that her son, Jesus,
Could read the Bible through,
Could read the Bible through. *Chorus*

The very next blessing that Mary had,
It was the blessing of three,
To know that her son, Jesus,
Could make the blind see,
Could make the blind see. *Chorus*

The very next blessing that Mary had,
It was the blessing of four,
To know that her son, Jesus,
Would live to help the poor,
Would live to help the poor. *Chorus*

The very next blessing that Mary had,
It was the blessing of five,
To know that her son, Jesus,
Could bring the dead alive,
Could bring the dead alive, *Chorus*

The very next blessing that Mary had,
It was the blessing of seven,
To know that her son, Jesus,
Was safe at last in heaven,
Was safe at last in heaven. *Chorus*

Mary counted her blessings,
She counted them one by one,
She found that her greatest blessing
Was her Godly son,
Was her Godly son. *Chorus*

THE CHERRY TREE CAROL

Jean Ritchie, traditional ballad-singer and dulcimer player from Viper, Kentucky, recalls her uncle Jason's comments about this song: "Now, have you ever hear that'n about Mary and Joseph and the argument over the cherry tree? Well, that's a kind of a quare song, a little story that never got printed in the Bible, but it got *told* by a whole lot of folks, and might be true, don't you know?" (From *Folk Songs of the Southern Appalachians as sung by Jean Ritchie,* Oak Publications, 1965)

When Jo-seph was an old man, An old man was he, He mar-ried Vir-gin Ma-ry, The Queen of Gal-i-lee, He mar-ried Vir-gin Ma-ry, The Queen of Gal-i-lee.

—— 2 ——

Then Mary spoke to Joseph,
So meek and so mild,
"Joseph, gather me some cherries,
For I am with child.
Joseph, gather me some cherries,
For I am with child."

—— 3 ——

Then Joseph grew in anger,
In anger grew he:
"Let the father of the thy baby
Gather cherries for thee.
Let the father of the thy baby
Gather cherries for thee."

—— 4 ——

Then Jesus spoke a few words,
A few words spoke He:
"Let my mother have some cherries,
Bow low down, cherry tree!
Let my mother have some cherries,
Bow low down, cherry tree!"

—— 5 ——

The cherry tree bowed down,
Bowed low down to the ground,
And Mary gathered cherries
While Joseph stood around,
And Mary gathered cherries
While Joseph stood around.

—— 6 ——

Then Joseph took Mary
All on his right knee.
"What have I done, oh, Lord,
Have mercy on me,
What have I done, oh, Lord,
Have mercy on me,

HAT MONTH WAS MY JESUS BORN IN?

This Negro Christmas song comes to us from one of the great traditional singers of our time—Vera Hall Ward. It was recorded by folklorist Harold Courlander while on a folk song collecting field trip in Alabama in 1950.

Tell me what month was my Je - sus born in?
He was born in an ox - stall man - ger,
I'm talking 'bout — Mar - y's Ba - by,

Last month of the

year.___

Tell me what month was my Je - sus born in?
He was born in an ox - stall man - ger,
I'm talking 'bout — Mar - y's Ba - by,

Last ___ month of the year. Well, you got Jan - u - ar - y,

O, HOW A ROSE E'ER BLOOMING

Michael Praetorious (1571-1621), German musical scholar and composer.
His musical output was voluminous, both in religious and secular works.
He is perhaps best known for his *Syntagma Musicum* ("Musical Treatise"),
a sort of music encyclopedia which dealt with choral and instrumental
music, musical instruments, music theory and counterpoint.

Michael Praetorious

Lo, how a Rose e'er bloom - ing, From ten - der stem ___ has sprung! Of Jes - se's lin - eage com - ing, As men of old ___ have sung. It came, a flow'r - et bright,

MAY NO EBB STAY THE FLOW OF THIS THRICE-HAPPY YULE-TIDE!

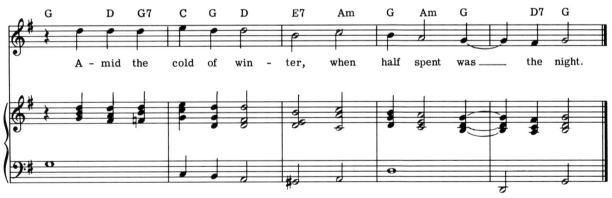

A - mid the cold of win - ter, when half spent was ___ the night.

—— 2 ——

Isaiah 'twas foretold it,
The rose I have in mind,
With Mary we behold it,
The Virgin Mother kind.
To show God's love aright,
She bore to men a Saviour,
When half-spent was the night.

GATHER AROUND THE CHRISTMAS TREE

John H. Hopkins came from a distinguished family of English musicians. He was a composer and organist in a number of churches, including the Rochester Cathedral, a post he held from 1856 until his death in 1900.

John Hopkins
(1822-1900)

CHORUS

G7　　C　　D　　E7　　Am　　　D7　　　　　G　　Em　Am　G　　Am7　D7　G

Ho - san - na, ho - san - na, ho - san - na in the high est!

— 2 —

Gather around the Christmas tree!
Gather around the Christmas tree!
Once the pride of the mountainside,
Now cut down to grace our Christmastide;
For Christ from heav'n to earth came down
To gain through death a nobler crown. *Chorus*

— 3 —

Gather around the Christmas tree!
Gather around the Christmas tree!
Every bough has a burden now,
They are gifts of love for us, we trow;
For Christ is born, His love to show,
And give good gifts to men below. *Chorus*

HOLY NIGHT

Adam was celebrated for his many operas, which were often performed at the Opera-Comique in Paris. He also wrote Church music, of which this is an example.

Adolphe Adam
(1803-1856)

O ho - ly night! _____ The stars are bright - ly shin - ing, It is the night of the dear Sav-iour's birth. Long lay the world _____ in sin and er - ror pin - ing, Till He ap-

C#m · G#7 · C#m · E7

peared and the soul felt its worth. A thrill of hope the

A · E7 · A

wear-y world re-joic-es, For yon-der breaks a new and glo-rious morn.

(over)

HEARD THE BELLS ON CHRISTMAS DAY

John Baptiste Calkin (born in London, 1827, date of death unknown) was a prolific composer of church services and anthems. The poetry of Henry Wadsworth Longfellow (1807-1882) was well known and highly regarded in England due to his voyages abroad and his publication there.

Henry W. Longfellow

J. Baptiste Calkin

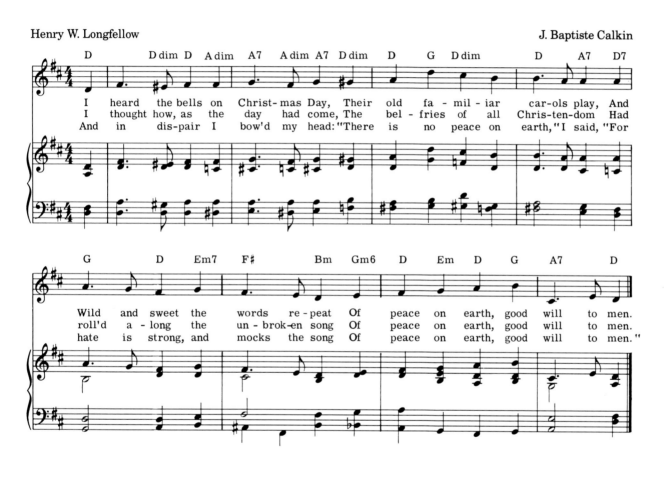

Verse lyrics:

I heard the bells on Christ-mas Day, Their old fa-mil-iar car-ols play, And
I thought how, as the day had come, The bel-fries of all Chris-ten-dom Had
And in dis-pair I bow'd my head: "There is no peace on earth," I said, "For

Wild and sweet the words re-peat Of peace on earth, good will to men.
roll'd a-long the un-brok-en song Of peace on earth, good will to men.
hate is strong, and mocks the song Of peace on earth, good will to men."

——— 4 ———

Then pealed the bells more loud and deep: "God is not dead, nor doth He sleep;
The wrong shall fail, the right prevail, With peace on earth, good will to men."

49

GO TELL IT ON THE MOUNTAIN

The Negro spirituals comprise a body of music of extraordinary beauty and variety. As an expression of the deep desires of oppressed people and the hope of common folk, their depth of vision and musical richness make them as alive and meaningful as when they were first sung. The birth of Christ represents not only the coming of the Redeemer, but the arrival of the Deliverer.

When I was a learn-er, I sought both night and day, I asked the Lord to aid me and He showed me the way.

CHORUS

Go tell it on the moun-tains, O-ver the hills and ev-'ry-where,—

Go tell it on the moun - tains, Our Je - sus Christ is born.

— 2 —

While shepherds kept their watching
O'er silent flocks by night,
Behold, throughout the heavens
There shone a holy light.   *Chorus*

— 3 —

The shepherds feared and trembled,
When, lo, above the earth
Rang out the angels' chorus,
That hailed our Saviour's birth.   *Chorus*

— 4 —

Down in a lowly manger,
Our humble Christ was born,
And God sent us salvation
That blessed Christmas morn.   *Chorus*

SAW THREE SHIPS

The three Magi arrived on their camels, "the ships of the desert"... This could be one interpretation of this old English carol, which dates back at least five hundred years. There is also an old legend about three mysterious ships sailing by, sometimes bearing gifts, sometimes bearing the holy family.

52

—— 2 ——

—— 3 ——

And what was in those ships all three,
On Christmas Day, on Christmas Day;
And what was in those ships all three,
On Christmas Day in the morning.

The Virgin Mary and Christ were there,
On Christmas Day, on Christmas Day;
The Virgin Mary and Christ were there,
On Christmas Day in the morning.

MARY HAD A BABY

A traditional Negro Christmas song. The image of the train is closely associated with salvation in many spirituals, as in, "Get on board, little children, there's room for many-a more."

Mar-y had a Ba-by, Oh, Lord, ___

Mar-y had a Ba-by, Oh, my ___ Lord. Mar-y had a Ba-by,

Oh, Lord, ___ The peo-ple keep a com-ing and the train ___ done gone.

—— 2 ——

What did she name Him?, Oh, Lord;
She called Him Jesus, Oh, my Lord;
Where was He born?, Oh, Lord;
The people keep a-coming and the train done gone.

—— 3 ——

Born in a stable, Oh, Lord;
Where did they lay Him?, Oh, my Lord;
Laid Him in a manger, Oh, Lord;
The people keep a-coming and the train done gone.

GOOD CHRISTIAN MEN, REJOICE

A German carol of the fourteenth century, originally written half in Latin and half in German. Scottish poet and religious reformer John Wedderburn (1500-1556), having been accused of heresy in 1539, was forced to flee to Wittenberg. There he came into contact with Lutheran hymns and translated this song into English. It was published in 1540 in Scotland after the death of James V in the *Compendious Book of Psalms and Spiritual Songs.*

Good Christ-ian men, re-joice_____ with heart and soul and voice,_____

Give ye heed to what we say: News! News! Je-sus Christ is born to-day!

Ox and ass be-fore Him bow, And He is in the man-ger now.

| B♭ | A7 | Dm | C7 | F | C7 | F |

Christ is born to - day, _____ Christ is born to - day! _____

— 2 —

Good Christian men, rejoice
With heart and soul and voice,
Now ye hear of endless bliss;
Joy! Joy! Jesus Christ was born for this.
He hath ope'd the heav'nly door,
And man is blessed evermore;
Christ was born for this,
Christ was born for this.

— 3 —

Good Christian men, rejoice
With heart and soul and voice,
Now ye need not fear the grave:
Peace! Peace! Jesus Christ was born to save.
Calls you one and calls you all,
To gain His everlasting hall;
Christ was born to save,
Christ was born to save.

IT WAS POOR LITTLE JESUS

A good example of a "leader-response" spiritual—with the leader telling the story and the congregation joining in with "yes, yes".

It was poor___ lit-tle Je - sus, Yes, yes,___ He was

born___ on ___ Christ - mas, Yes, yes,___ And ___

laid ___ in a man - ger, Yes, yes;___

CHORUS

Was - n't that a pit - y and a shame? Lord, Lord, ___

Was - n't that a pit - y and a shame? _____

— 2 —

Poor little Jesus, Yes, yes,
Child of Mary, Yes, yes,
Didn't have no cradle, Yes, yes,   *Chorus*

— 3 —

Poor little Jesus, Yes, yes,
They took Him from a manger, Yes, yes,
They took Him from his mother, Yes, yes,   *Chorus*

— 4 —

Poor little Jesus, Yes, yes,
They bound Him with a halter, Yes, yes,
And whipped Him up the mountain, Yes, yes,   *Chorus*

— 5 —

Poor little Jesus, Yes, yes,
They nailed Him to the cross, Lord, Yes, yes,
They hung Him with a robber, Yes, yes,   *Chorus*

— 6 —

Poor little Jesus, Yes, yes,
He's risen from darkness, Yes, yes,
He's ascended into glory, Yes, yes,   *Chorus*

— 7 —

Poor little Jesus, Yes, yes,
Born on Friday, Yes, yes,
Born on Christmas, Yes, yes,   *Chorus*

IT TOOK PLACE ONE CHRISTMAS EVE

A sixteenth-century carol from the Champagne region of France. The word, "Noé" is an old variation of Noel.

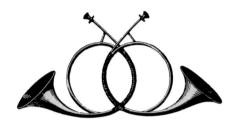

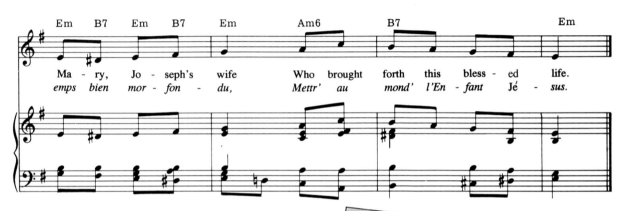

Ma - ry, Jo - seph's wife | Who brought forth this bless - ed life.
emps bien mor - fon - du, | *Mettr' au mond' l'En - fant Jé - sus.*

—— 2 ——

And the shepherds, they all came (2)
Singing praises to His name. (2)
They brought gifts of drink and food
To the Holy Child, so good;
Simple gifts, like milk and cheese,
Hoping thus the Child to please.

Les bergers vinr' par douzaines (2)
Lui apporter leurs aubaines. (2)
L'un lui apporter à boire,
L'autr' lui apporter des poires,
Ou bien un bol de laitage,
Ou bien cinq ou six fromages.

—— 3 ——

Joseph, gazing to the skies, (2)
Just could not believe his eyes. (2)
He looked at the Child with love;
The true Son of God above,
Hiding His divinity
Under his humanity.

Saint-Joseph, à deux genoux, (2)
N'en veut pas croir' ses deux yeux, (2)
Il r'gardait l'divin Enfant,
Le vrai fis du Dieu vivant,
Cachant sa divinité
Pard'ssous son humanité.

TONIGHT A CHILD IS BORN

A Spanish Christmas song from Santañilla Province.

English text
by J.S.

Spain

On this eve - ning   came an In - fant   born in - to the   win - ter's sting,   If I on - ly,   my dear Ba - by,   could but clothe You   like a King.

Es - ta no - che   na - ce un Ni - ño   en - tre la es - car - cha y el hie - lo.   Quien pu - die - ra,   Ni - ño mi - o,   ves - tir - te de   ter - cio pe - lo.   {A - le

gri, a - le - gri, a - le - gri-a,   A - le - gri, a - le - gri   What de-
                                                                      que pla-

light!   For to us a   Child is giv - en,   born in
cer!   *Es - ta no - che* *na - ce un Ni - ño* *en el*

Beth - le - hem this night.____   A - le - night.____
por - ta *de Be - lén* ____   *lén.* ____

— 2 —

Oh, the Virgin, she is washing
With a little bit of soap.
And her hands are getting roughened,
Hands that hold all mankind's hope.   *Chorus*

La Virgen está lavando
Con un poco de jabón.
Se le picaron las manos,
Manos de mi corazón.   *Chorus*

JOYFUL SING YE, CHRISTIAN PEOPLE

Andreas Hammerschmidt (1612-1675) was an Austro-Bohemian organist and composer. In 1646 he published a collection of *Geistliche Motetten und Concerten,* in which this hymn appears. In 1723 J.S. Bach set this composition for four-part chorale in his Cantata 40, *Dazu ist erscheinen der Sohn Gottes.* I have extracted the melody as a solo voice and have transposed the piece to E minor from Bach's F minor (without otherwise changing Bach's arrangement).

J.S. Bach

Joy - ful sing, ye Chris - tian peo - ple, Loud re-joice with one ac-cord,
Je - sus, let Thou Thine e -lec - ted fur - ther in Thy fa - vor fare,

Hail ye Je - sus Christ the Lord, Sound the chimes from ev - 'ry stee - ple
Hear Thou them and grant their pray'r, Quick - en all who are de - ject - ed

Deck the hearth with hol - ly gay, For to - day is Christ-mas Day.
Give Thy folk all gath - ered here, Peace and joy this com - ing year.

Through the world glad tid - ings ring - ing, Joy - ful mul - ti - tudes are sing - ing:
Joy - ful, joy - ful dawns the mor - row, Christ has ban - ished ev - 'ry sor - row,

Glo - ry, glo - ry to the High - est, Peace on earth, good will to all men.
Rap - ture, rap - ture ev - er near - ing, See the Son of Grace ap - pear - ing.

THE VIRGIN MARY HAD A-ONE SON

A Christmas gospel-lullaby.

The ___ Vir ___ gin ___ Mar - y   had a - one Son, ___

CHORUS

Mm ___ mm,   Glo - ry hal - le - lu - jah,   mm ___ mm

Pret - ty lit - tle Ba - by,   Glo ___ ry be   to   the   new - born   King.

— 2 —

Mary, what you gonna name
that pretty little baby?   *Chorus*

— 3 —

Some call Him one thing,
think I'll name Him Jesus,   *Chorus*

— 4 —

Some call Him one thing,
think I'll name Him Emmanuel,   *Chorus*

SANTA CLAUS BLUES

Blues at Christmas? Why not? Not everyone is surrounded by loving family and friends during the holiday season. This blues was heard at the Central State Prison Farm at Sugarland, Texas, in 1941.

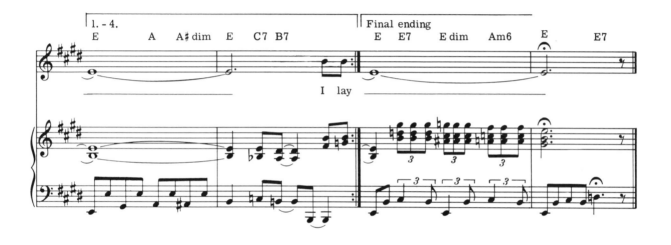

— 2 —

I lay down last night, turning from side to side,
I lay down last night, turning from side to side,
I was not sick, I was just dissatisfied.

— 3 —

I got up this morning, blues walking 'round my bed,
I got up this morning, blues walking 'round my bed,
Went to eat my breakfast, blues was all in my bread.

— 4 —

Well, tomorrow's Christmas and I want to see Santa Claus,
Well, tomorrow's Christmas and I want to see Santa Claus,
If I don't get my baby for Christmas, gonna break all the laws.

— 5 —

Santy Claus, Santy Claus, listen to my plea,
Santy Claus, Santy Claus, listen to my plea,
I don't want nothin' for Christmas but my baby back to me.

SILENT NIGHT, HOLY NIGHT

Franz Xaver Gruber (1787-1863), Austrian church organist and composer.
A few days before Christmas 1818 the church organ broke down. Gruber
tells us: "On December 24, 1818, the then curate of the newly created parish
of Oberndorf, Mr. Joseph Mohr, gave me a poem which he requested me to
set for suitable music, for two solo voices, chorus and guitar accompani-
ment. The same evening I brought him the desired simple composition,
which that same holy evening was sung with much success."

Joseph Mohr   Franz Gruber

Si - lent night, ho - ly night,
Stil - le Nacht hei - li - ge Nacht!

All is calm, all is bright.
Al - les schlaft, ein - sam wacht.

'Round yon Vir - gin Moth - er and Child,
Nur das trau - te hoch - hei - li - ge Paar,

D   **D♯ dim**   **A**

Ho - ly In - fant, so ten - der and mild,
Hol - der Kna - be mit lok - ki - gem Haar,

E   **E7**   **F♯m**   **F♯m6**

Sleep in heav - en - ly peace, _____
Schlaf in himm - li - scher Ruh, _____

A   **E7**   **A**

Sleep in heav - en - ly peace. _____
Schlaf in himm - le - scher Ruh. _____

—— 2 ——

Silent night, holy night!
Shepherds quake at the sight,
Glories stream from heaven afar,
Heav'nly hosts sing alleluia;
Christ the Saviour is born!
Christ the Saviour is born!

Stille Nacht, heilige Nacht!
Hirten erst kund gemacht;
Durch der Engel Halleluja
Tönt es laut von fern und nah:
Christ, der Retter, ist da!
Christ, der Retter, ist da!

—— 3 ——

Silent night, holy night!
Wondrous star, lend thy light!
With the angels let us sing
Alleluia to our King!
Christ the Saviour is here,
Jesus the Saviour is here!

Stille Nacht, heilige Nacht!
Gottes Sohn, O wie lacht
Lieb' aus deinem göttlichen Mund,
Da uns schlägt die rettende Stund',
Christ in deiner Geburt,
Christ in deiner Geburt!

71

COME, ALL YE FAITHFUL

The Portuguese embassy in London in the eighteenth century was the site of the performance of many fine Catholic hymns. It was there that *Adeste Fidelis* was probably first sung in England. This was later translated as *O Come, All Ye Faithful*. The original manuscript is in the hand of a music copyist named J.F. Wade (1711-1786), and it was he who probably wrote the music which he later published in his *Cantus Diversi*.

O come, all ye faith - ful, joy - ful and tri - um - phant, O come ye, O come ye to Beth - le hem. Come and be hold Him, born the King of An - gels.

CHORUS

O come, let us a - dore Him, O come, let us a - dore Him, O

come, let us a - dore Him, ___ Christ ___ the Lord.

—— 2 ——

Sing chorus of angels, sing in exultation
O sing all ye citizens of heaven above!
Glory to God, all glory in the highest;   *Chorus*

—— 3 ——

Yea Lord, we greet thee, born this happy morning
Jesus, to thee be all glory giv'n;
Word of the Father. Now in flesh appearing;   *Chorus*

—— 4 ——

Adeste fidele,
Laeti triumphantes,
Venite, venite in Bethlehem.
Natum videte,
Regem angleorum,
Venite, adoremus,
Venite, adoremus,
Venite, adoremus Dominum.

CHILD THIS DAY IS BORN

First published in 1833 in William Sandys' *Christmas Carols, Ancient and Modern, including the most popular in the West of England, with the tunes to which they are sung.*

A Child this day is born, A Child of high renown, Most worthy of a scep-tre, A scep-tre and a crown.

CHORUS

Now-ell, Now-ell, Now-ell, Now-ell sing all we may, Be-

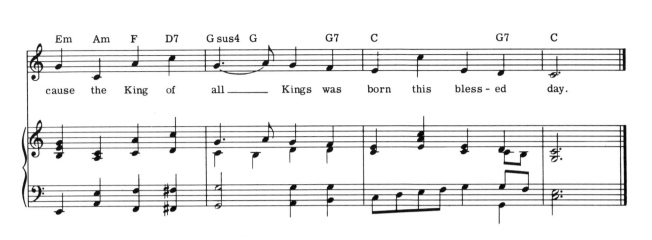

cause   the   King   of   all _____ Kings   was   born   this   bless - ed   day.

—— 2 ——

These tidings shepherds heard,
In fields watching their fold,
Were by an angel unto them
That night revealed and told.   *Chorus*

—— 3 ——

To whom the angel spoke,
Saying, "Be not afraid;
Be glad, poor silly shepherds—
Why are you so dismayed?"   *Chorus*

—— 4 ——

"For lo! I bring you tidings
Of gladness and of mirth,
Which cometh to all people by
This Holy Infant's birth":   *Chorus*

—— 5 ——

Then was there with the angel
An host incontinent
Of heavenly bright soldiers,
Which from the Highest was sent: *Chorus*

—— 6 ——

Lauding the Lord of God,
And his celestial King;
All glory be in Paradise,
This heavenly host did sing: *Chorus*

—— 7 ——

And as the angel told them,
So to them did appear;
They found the young Child, Jesus Christ
With Mary, His mother dear: *Chorus*

GOD REST YOU MERRY GENTLEMEN

We find versions of this old carol dating back to
sixteenth-century England.

God rest you mer-ry gen-tle-men, Let noth-ing you dis-may, Re-
mem-ber Christ our Sav-i-or Was born on Christ-mas

Day, To save us all from Sa-tan's pow'r, When we have gone a-stray.

—— 2 ——

From God our heav'nly Father,
A blessed Angel came,
And unto certain shepherds
Brought tidings of the same;
How that in Bethlehem was born
The Son of God by Name. *Chorus*

—— 3 ——

The Shepherds at those tidings
Rejoiced much in mind
And left their flocks a-feeding
In tempest, storm, and wind,
And went straightway to Bethlehem
The Son of God to find. *Chorus*

CHORUS

Oh,— ti - dings of com — fort and joy, com-fort and joy, Oh,—

ti — dings of com — fort and joy.

— 4 —

And when they came to Bethlehem,
Where our dear Savior lay,
They found Him in a manger
Where oxen feed on hay;
His mother Mary kneeling down
Unto the Lord did pray.   *Chorus*

— 5 —

Now to the Lord sing praises,
All you within this place,
And with true love and brotherhood
Each other now embrace;
This holy tide of Christmas
All other doth deface.   *Chorus*

THE FIRST NOËL

First published in William Sandys' 1833 collection
(cf. *A Child This Day Is Born*). It would seem to be much
older than this— perhaps as much as two hundred
years, originating in France.

The first Noel the angels did say, Was to
cer - tain poor shep - herds in fields as they lay; In
fields where they lay keep - ing their sheep On a

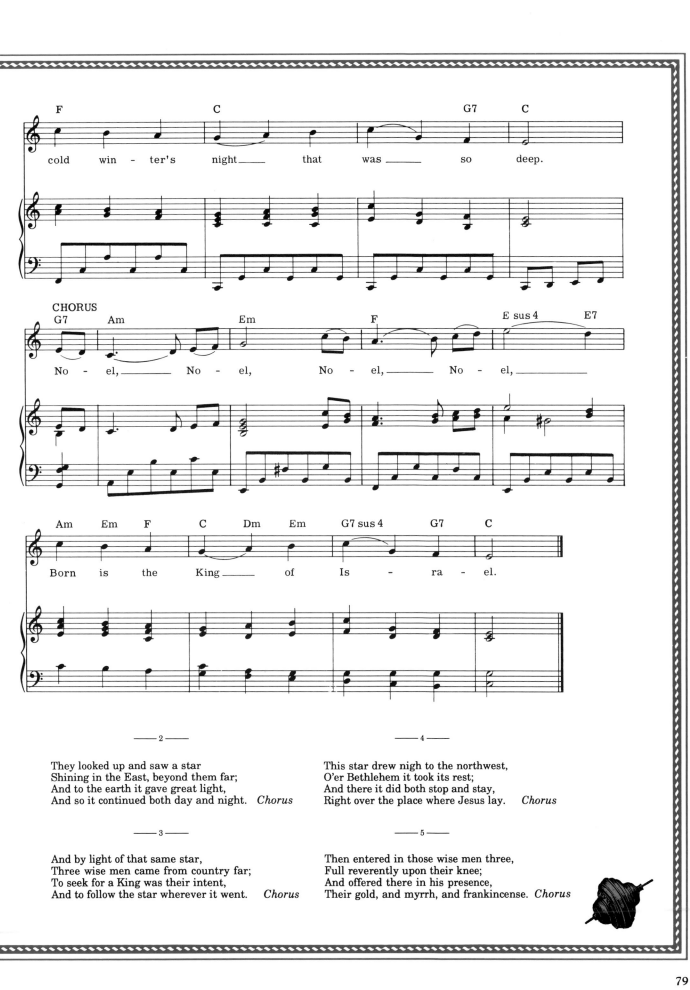

F		C			G7	C

cold win - ter's night ____ that was ____ so deep.

CHORUS

G7	Am	Em	F	E sus 4	E7

No - el, ____ No - el, No - el, ____ No - el, ____

Am	Em	F	C	Dm	Em	G7 sus 4	G7	C

Born is the King ____ of Is - ra - el.

— 2 —

They looked up and saw a star
Shining in the East, beyond them far;
And to the earth it gave great light,
And so it continued both day and night. *Chorus*

— 3 —

And by light of that same star,
Three wise men came from country far;
To seek for a King was their intent,
And to follow the star wherever it went. *Chorus*

— 4 —

This star drew nigh to the northwest,
O'er Bethlehem it took its rest;
And there it did both stop and stay,
Right over the place where Jesus lay. *Chorus*

— 5 —

Then entered in those wise men three,
Full reverently upon their knee;
And offered there in his presence,
Their gold, and myrrh, and frankincense. *Chorus*

E ALL GO TO BETHLEHEM

This is based on a French carol whose melody is more reminiscent of Prague than Paris. Children singing it are encouraged to imitate by sound and movement the instrument being sung about. They should also make up additional verses with other names, instruments, sounds and movements.

D   **Em**   **A7**   **D**   **Bm**

in His cra - dle.   Sing and ___ play on   Christ-mas ___ Day.

rons   tout   doux   oui,   Doux   No - ël,   bel   En - fant,

Em   **A7**   **D**   **D.C.**

We will rock ___ Him ___ ten - der - ly.

Nous   Le   ber - ce - rons   gai - ment.

D.C.
(last time al Fine)

—— 2 ——

Jacky, won't you play your pipes?
Nyah, nyah, nyah, nyah, nyah, nyah, nyah.   *Chorus*

Toi, Jacquot, prends ta musette...

—— 3 ——

Jeannie, come and play your flute.
Doodle, doodle, doodle, doo.   *Chorus*

Et toi, Jeannot, ton flutiau...

—— 4 ——

Nicholas will bring his bass.
Zum, zum, zum, zum, zum, zum, zum.   *Chorus*

Nicolas prendra sa basse...

—— 5 ——

Jerry will strum his guitar.
Plunk, plunk, plunk, plunk, plunk, plunk.   *Chorus*

Jerry jouera sa guitare...

In all, 364 gifts were given—12 partridges, 22 turtle doves, 30 French hens, 36 calling birds, 40 golden rings, 42 geese, 42 swans, 40 milkmaids, 36 pipers, 30 drummers, 22 lords and 12 ladies!

DECK THE HALLS

This spirited and jovial secular carol comes to us from Wales.

Deck the halls with boughs of hol-ly,
'Tis the sea-son to be jol-ly.
Fa la la la la, la la la la.

Don we now our gay ap-par-el, Fa la la, la la la, la la la.

Troll the an-cient yule-tide ca-rol; Fa la la la la, la la la la.

— 2 —

See the blazing yule before us,
Fa la la la la la la la la,
Strike the harp, and join the chorus,
Fa la la la la la la la la,
Follow me in merry measure,
Fa ia la la la la la la la,
While I tell of Christmas treasure,
Fa la la la la la la la la.

— 3 —

Fast away the old year passes,
Fa la la la la la la la la,
Hail the new! ye lads and lasses,
Fa la la la la la la la la,
Sing we joyous all together,
Fa la la la la la la la la,
Heedless of the wind and weather,
Fa la la la la la la la la.

LITTLE TOWN OF BETHLEHEM

When Phillips Brooks (1835-1893) visited Bethlehem in 1866, he was so moved that he wrote these verses upon his return for the Christmas services in the Sunday School at Holy Trinity in Philadelphia, where he was rector. The church organist, Lewis H. Redner (1831-1908) immediately set it to music. Brooks ended his days as Bishop of Boston. Upon his death it was said, "not since Lincoln was any man so widely mourned".

Phillips Brooks

Lewis H. Redner

O lit - tle town of Beth - le - hem, How still we see thee lie! A-

bove thy deep and dream-less sleep The si - lent stars go by; Yet

in thy dark streets shin - eth The ev - er - last - ing Light; The

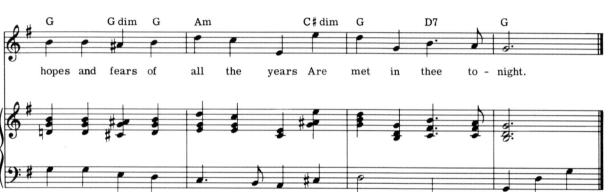

| G | G dim | G | Am | | C# dim | G | | D7 | | G |

hopes and fears of all the years Are met in thee to - night.

——— 2 ———

For Christ is born of Mary,
And gathered all above,
While mortals sleep, the angels keep
Their watch of wondering love.
O morning stars, together
Proclaim the holy birth,
And praises sing to God the King,
And peace to men on earth.

——— 3 ———

How silently, how silently,
The wondrous gift is giv'n!
So God imparts to human hearts
The blessings of His heav'n.
No ear may hear His coming,
But in this world of sin,
Where meek souls will receive Him still,
The dear Christ enters in.

——— 4 ———

O holy Child of Bethlehem,
Descend to us, we pray,
Cast out our sin and enter in,
Be born in us today.
We hear the Christmas angels
The great glad tidings tell,
O come to us, abide with us,
Our Lord, Emmanuel.

GOOD KING WENCESLAS

The tune is originally that of an old spring carol, *Tempus adest floridium*.
In 1853, John Mason Neale (1818-1856), English divine and scholar, who
is known principally for his translations of ancient and medieval hymns,
used this melody in his retelling of the legend of Good King Wenzel,
King of Bohemia from 928 to 935, who was revered for his many acts of
kindness toward the poor.

Good King Wen - ces - las looked out, On the feast of Ste - phen,
When the snow lay round a - bout, deep and crisp and e - ven.

Bright - ly shone the moon that night, Though the frost was cru - el,

When a poor man came in sight, Gath -'ring win - ter fu - el.

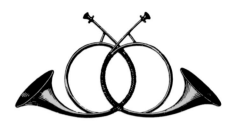

——— 2 ———

"Hither, page, and stand by me,
If thou know'st it telling,
Yonder peasant, who is he?
Where and what his dwelling?"
"Sire, he lives a good league hence,
Underneath the mountain,
Right against the forest fence,
By Saint Agnes' fountain."

——— 3 ———

"Bring me flesh, and bring me wine,
Bring me pine-logs hither:
Thou and I shall see him dine,
When we bear them thither."
Page and monarch, forth they went,
Forth they went together;
Through the rude wind's wild lament,
And the bitter weather.

——— 4 ———

"Sire, the night is darker now,
And the wind grows stronger;
Fails my heart, I know not how;
I can go no longer."
"Mark my footsteps, my good page,
Tread thou in them boldly;
Thou shalt find the winter's rage
Freeze thy blood less coldly."

——— 5 ———

In his master's steps he trod,
Where the snow lay dinted;
Heat was in the very sod
Which the Saint had printed.
Therefore, Christian men, be sure,
Wealth or rank possessing,
Ye who now will bless the poor,
Shall yourselves find blessing.

WAY IN A MANGER

In 1786, the Scottish composer, Alexander Hume set to music a love poem by Robert Burns, entitled, *Flow Gently, Sweet Afton.* It was to this beautiful melody that this translation of a poem attributed to Martin Luther was set by Jonathan E. Spillman.

A - way in a—— man-ger, no crib for His bed, The lit - tle Lord Je - sus lay down His sweet head. The stars in the— heav - ens looked down where He lay, The lit - tle Lord Je - sus a - sleep in the hay. The——

cat - tle are low - ing, the poor Ba - by wakes, But little Lord

Je - sus no cry - ing He makes; I love Thee, Lord Je - sus, look

down from the sky, And stay by my cra - dle to watch lul - a - by.

— 2 —

Be near me, Lord Jesus, I ask Thee to stay
Close by me forever and love me, I pray.
Bless all the dear children in Thy tender care,
And take us to heaven to live with Thee there.

— 3 —

Away in a manger, no crib for His bed,
The little Lord Jesus lay down His sweet head.
The stars in the heavens looked down where He lay,
The little Lord Jesus, asleep in the hay.

IT CAME UPON THE MIDNIGHT CLEAR

Edmund H. Sears (1810-1876) was a Massachusetts Unitarian clergyman and editor of the *Monthly Religious Magazine.* However, these verses were first published in the *Christian Register* in 1850. In that same year, Richard S. Willis (1819-1900), composed this tune, entitling it simply *Christmas Carol.* After some years Sears' words and Willis' music combined to create one of the most popular carols in the English language.

Edmund H. Sears

Richard S. Willis

It came up-on the mid - night clear, That glo - ri - ous
through the clo - ven skies they come, With peace - ful
lo, the days are hast - 'ning on, By pro - phet -

song of old, From an - gels bend - ing
wings un - furled; And still their heav - en - ly
bards fore - told, When, with the ev - er

near the earth To touch their harps of gold.
mu - sic floats O'er all the wea - ry world:
cir - cling years, Comes 'round the age of gold:

Peace on the earth ____ good will to men From
A - bove its sad ____ and low - ly plains They
When peace shall o - ver all the earth It's

heav - en's all gra - cious King, _____ The world in
bend ____ on hov - er - ing wing, _____ And ev - er
an - cient splen - dors fling, _____ And the whole

sol - emn still - ness lay to hear the an - gels
o'er ____ its Ba - bel sounds The bless - ed an - gels
world ____ give back the song Which now the an - gels

1. 2.

sing. _____ (2) Still sing. _____
sing. _____ (3) For

Final ending

COME LITTLE CHILDREN

Johann Abraham Peter Schulz (1747-1800), German organist, conductor and composer. He was a prolific composer who wrote music for the stage, operas as well as sacred music. Today's Suzuki method violin students (and their parents) will instantly recognize this tune.

J. A. P. Schulz

O come, lit - tle chil - dren, from cot and from hall, O
Ihr kin - der - lein, kom - met, o kom - met doch all! Zur

come to the man - ger in Beth - le - hem's stall. There
krip - pe her kom - met in Beth - le - hems stall. Und

meek - ly He li - eth, the heav - en - ly Child, So
seht was in dies - er hoch - heil - i - gen Nacht. Der

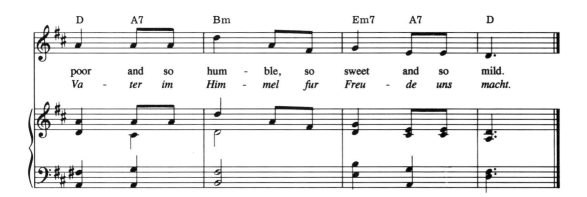

| D | A7 | Bm | | Em7 | A7 | D |

poor and so hum - ble, so sweet and so mild.
Va - ter im Him - mel für Freu - de uns macht.

— 2 —

The hay is His pillow, the manger His bed,
The beasts stand in wonder to gaze on His head,
Yet there where He lieth, so weak and so poor,
Come shepherds and wise men to kneel at His door.

Da liegt es, ach Kinder, auf Heu und auf Stroh,
Maria und Josef betrachten es froh;
Die redlichen Hirten knien betend davor,
Hoch oben schwebt jubelnd der Engelein Chor.

— 3 —

Now "Glory to God!" sing the angels on high,
And "Peace upon earth!" heav'nly voices reply.
Then come, little children, and join in the lay
That gladdened the world on that first Christmas Day.

O beugt, wie die Hirten, anbetend die Knie,
Erhebet die Händlein und danket wie sie!
Stimmt freudig, ihr Kinder, wer sollt' sich nicht freu'n?
Stimmt freudig zum Jubel der Engel mit ein.

AULD LANG SYNE

It is by his songs that Robert Burns (1759-1796) is best known, and it is his songs that have carried his reputation around the world. Burn's aim was to recover as many airs and sets of words as he could, and to re-create, where necessary, the song in the true spirit of the Scottish folk tradition. Although attributed to him, Burns never claimed *Auld Lang Syne.* He was content to describe it simply as an old fragment he discovered.

Robert Burns

Should auld ac-quain-tance be for-got and___ nev-er brought to mind? Should

auld ac-quain-tance be for-got and___ days of auld lang syne?

CHORUS

For auld___ lang___ syne, my dear, for auld___ lang___ syne, We'll

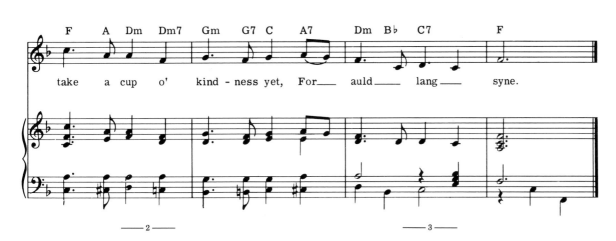

take a cup o' kind-ness yet, For___ auld___ lang___ syne.

—— 2 ——

We twa ha'e ran aboot the braes
And pu'd the gowans fine,
We've wandered many a weary foot
Sin auld lang syne.   *Chorus*

—— 3 ——

We twa ha'e sported i' the burn
Frae mornin' sun till dine,
But seas between us braid ha'e roared
Sin auld lang syne.   *Chorus*

—— 4 ——

And here's a hand my trusty friend,
And gie's a hand o' thine;
We'll tak' a cup o' kindness yet
For auld lang syne.   *Chorus*